Shugborough Inscription

Wordplay for the Lords and Ladies

Dan Mento

ISBN-13: 978-0-9996397-4-0

Introduction
O·U·O·S·V·A·V·V
D·   M·

Deep within the rolling hills of Staffordshire, amidst the English countryside, lies Shugborough Hall, an estate with a folly known as the Shepherd's Monument.

This monument features a cryptic ten-letter inscription perplexing code breakers and treasure hunters for centuries. The inscription is a carved tablet mounted on a wall with a beautiful copy of Nicolas Poussin's artwork,

The Arcadian Shepherds by Peter Scheemakers was sculpted above the tablet. The tablet and sculpture are within a stone arch resembling a cave mouth between two pillars.

The Shugborough Shepherd's Inscription, a puzzle of ten letters and nine dots, has long been a source of intrigue. It often distracts viewers from the monument's true mystery, which lies within Nicolas Poussin's masterpiece, *The Arcadian Shepherds*.

The shepherd's fingers, subtly pointing towards the letters N and R in the Latin phrase "*Et In Arcadia Ego,*" reveal the inscription's author and the monument's dedication. This phrase is placed in a seemingly idyllic scene, with its funerary sculptured art hidden amongst pastoral beauty, which hints at the ever-present shadow of mortality.

The Shugborough Shepherd's Monument is a treasure trove of three distinct ciphers. The first is a ten-letter wordplay solution, a testament to the fleeting nature of life and the enduring power of language. The second solution is a geometric construct that, by plotting the dots that follow the letters in the inscription, forms the planet Saturn, revealing the monument's designer. The third solution is an anagrammatic of *Et In Arcadia Ego*, a four-century-old enigma that unveils the hidden secret of Poussin's painting *The Arcadian Shepherds*. It reveals the three Goddesses –Archaic Latin Deai, Greek Gaia, and Greek Ceto-alluding to the author of the Shugborough Shepherd's inscription and the monument's dedication. Over time, many stories have circulated about the inscription holding the key to hidden treasures, such as Spanish gold, the Holy Grail, or Christ's bloodline.

While my findings may not have uncovered any buried Templar treasure or divine legacy, I have provided some insight into the minds of those who commissioned and admired this enigmatic monument. In these ways, the Shugborough code transformed the estate into a living intellectual playground, a testament to the enduring power of wordplay and the quest for knowledge hidden in veiled symbolism.

Chapter One
British Nobility
O·U·O·S·V·A·V·V

D·   M·

British society in the 18th century was a complex hierarchy with the peerage system as a central element, but wealth and social influence also played a significant role. The peerage system was created to differentiate between the aristocracy's different ranks, consisting of five levels: duke, marquess, earl, viscount, and baron. Members of the aristocracy enjoyed several privileges, such as exemption from certain taxes, the right to sit in the House of Lords, and the ability to hold high-ranking positions in the government and military.

George Anson, who was raised at Shugborough Hall, was awarded the title of 1st Baron after successfully sailing around the world despite harsh conditions and crew loss. This achievement was significant, as he captured the Spanish treasure ship *Nuestra Señora de Covadonga*. It is worth noting that the British nobility and aristocratic society played a fascinating and influential role in shaping Britain's culture, politics, economy, and the world during the 1700s. (Baker).

Grand British houses had transformed from impregnable fortresses like Warwick Castle to sprawling estates like Highclere Castle. Initially, castles rose as intimidating testaments to power, housing not just knights and lords but also government offices, armories, and even prisons. As warfare evolved and empires expanded, the need for such rigid defenses waned. English manor houses blossomed in their place, prioritizing comfort and elegance over battlements and drawbridges (Brain).

The 16th to 18th centuries witnessed the golden age of the country house. Flush with wealth extracted from vast landed estates; the aristocracy embarked on a magnificent building spree. Blenheim Palace's baroque grandeur, Chatsworth House's art-filled galleries, and Castle Howard's sprawling gardens exemplified the luxury of this era. These weren't simply homes but expressions of status, political influence, and refined taste. Within their walls, elaborate parties were hosted for dignitaries, hunting expeditions tested horsemanship and marksmanship, and artists crafted exquisite works, all under the watchful eyes of priceless antiquities and family portraits (Brain).

More than just bricks and mortar, these grand houses stand as testaments to a bygone era, whispering tales of power, privilege, and artistic patronage. They offer a glimpse into a world where wealth manifested in architectural masterpieces and social hierarchies were etched in every gilded room and manicured lawn. Even today, they continue to fascinate us, reminding us of the enduring legacy of England's grand architectural heritage. "The history of the English stately home offers a fascinating insight into the social interactions and conventions that played out in some of the grandest mansions across the country. These imposing estates would have hosted many historically significant events, celebrations, parties, and gatherings, turning them into social hubs" (Brain).

The aristocracy in England maintained their lavish lifestyles for generations by leasing land to farmers and other businesses. They benefited from laws that favored them, such as the entail, a form of legal trust that stipulated that houses and estates had to be passed down from father to son, amassing generational fortunes (Scheong). The British nobility flaunted their wealth and power through extravagant lifestyles and status symbols, such as rare and expensive artworks, books, jewels, and curiosities. Many nobles amassed vast collections of paintings, sculptures, manuscripts, maps, gems, and other objects of cultural and historical value. They hosted and attended extravagant parties, balls, masquerades, and gambling events. The nobility enjoyed various social activities that often involved dressing up in elaborate costumes, dancing, drinking, playing cards, and betting large sums of money. Many estates became bankrupt from endless celebrations, forcing many to sell possessions. Shugborough Hall was the same, selling artwork and furniture to pay their debts in 1842 (Scheong) (Smith).

During the opulent era of European aristocracy (1700s-1800s), the pineapple shone as the ultimate symbol of conspicuous consumption and worldly desire. It was not just a fruit but also a tropical treasure, with its spiky crown serving as a mark of exclusivity for the elite. The nobility did not simply consume this prickly prize; it graced their tables as a centerpiece, admired for its exotic beauty more than its fleeting flavor. The affluent, driven by their love for extravagance, even rented pineapples for special occasions, a temporary taste of forbidden luxury. The spoils of colonialism further enhanced the pineapple's aura, standing as a trophy from conquered lands, a tangible symbol of empire etched in its spiky skin. Its rarity fueled its value; imagine, a single pineapple in the American colonies could cost a staggering $8,000 in today's currency! Its perishability added to its allure, while its unfamiliarity whispered of distant voyages and sun-drenched shores (Moffat). Many estates in England boasted large greenhouses called pineries for growing pineapples. Cannon Hall, Castle Howard, Chatsworth, and Wentworth Woodhouse were among these estates. According to Moffat, "In 1825, a fine pineapple weighing 11¾ lbs. with a circumference of 2 feet was cut at Viscount Anson's home, Shugborough Hall. This fruit was believed to be the largest ever grown in Britain" (Moffat).

The pineapple was not just a fruit but also a potent symbol of wealth, power, and the intoxicating allure of the unknown. The obsession with pineapples led to their depiction in various forms of art and design. The affluent used pineapples to decorate napkins, tablecloths, wallpaper, and even bedposts to symbolize hospitality and generosity. The fruit became synonymous with opulence and wealth in 17th and 18th-century Europe. The pineapple's journey from South America to Europe by Spanish explorers in the 16th century further added to its allure. Europeans encountered the fruit for the first time in the Caribbean and South America, where they were captivated by its appearance, fragrance, and flavor. Descriptions of the pineapple by explorers and writers of the time were filled with admiration and hyperbole. The pineapple's association with luxury, rarity, and colonial conquest made it a highly prized symbol of social status in Europe. The pineapple's presence at social gatherings signified wealth and sophistication and would promote aristocratic distinction from others (Bell).

In addition to their fondness of the pineapple, the British aristocracy in the 1600s-1800s had a unique fascination for wordplay, particularly anagrams, which they considered a rarefied status symbol and a hallmark of cultural refinement. Anagrams, intricate word games that involve rearranging the letters of a word or phrase to create a new word or phrase, were their chosen form of intellectual expression. These games were not just a pastime but also a means to convey secret messages, display wit and intelligence, and maintain their position at the pinnacle of society. By engaging in anagrams, they demonstrated their wealth, power, sophistication, and exclusivity (Shortz). Creating clever word games and puzzles was considered a sign of intellectual aptitude and sophistication, and the ability to develop and solve anagrams was seen as a mark of distinction among the upper classes. Anagrams were also used to showcase one's knowledge of foreign languages, as they could be created using words from different languages. Individuals skilled at creating anagrams were known as anagrammatists, a sign of superior education (Shortz).

Apart from anagrams, other forms of wordplay, such as puns, riddles, and acrostics, were also popular among the aristocracy. These games were often played at social gatherings and dinner parties, where they served as a form of entertainment and intellectual stimulation.

Understanding the lives and skills of the artisans who crafted the monument is crucial to decoding its message. Were they reflecting the values of their patrons, subtly critiquing their excesses, or weaving their narratives into the stone? We aim to unravel its true purpose and reason only by immersing ourselves in the cultural context, the artisans' artistry, and the inscription's cryptic wordplay message. Anagrams were all the rage during this period, a fashionable, intimidating playground for the affluent to flex their mental muscles.

The British aristocracy favored material wealth, exemplified by their estates and fondness for the exotic pineapple. They also tended to celebrate their social status and distinguish themselves intellectually from their peers. These traits are evident in the Shepherd's Monument, an elaborate maze highlighting Thomas's superior intellect and honors his brother Admiral George Anson's accomplishments and friend Thomas Wright.

Believing the Shugborough inscription is a coded message for buried treasure, the bloodline of Christ, or the Holy Grail is unrealistic. Wealthy landowners like the Shugborough owners wouldn't leave vast riches hidden. It is unlikely for a secret society or holy lineage to be subtly announced. After all, if the inscription indeed held the key to immense wealth or a legendary artifact, the Anson family would have likely exploited it themselves, securing their financial future or leveraging the notoriety for social advancement.

Chapter Two
Shugborough Hall
O·U·O·S·V·A·V·V
D·   M·

(Jones and Co.)

Shugborough Hall, a 17th-century stately home nestled in the heart of Staffordshire, England, is a captivating testament to the beauty of nature and human ingenuity. The estate, owned by the National Trust, is a haven of parklands, woodlands, meadows, gardens, and a river. Its natural splendor is a magnet for tourists, who come to marvel at its notable follies, such as the Octagon Tower, the Ruins, the Arch of Adrian, the Temple of the Wind, the Lanthorn of Demosthenes (also known as the

Dark Lantern Monument), the Doric Temple, the Chinese House, the Cat's Monument, and the Shepherd's Monument.

Shugborough Hall was originally an Episcopal palace owned by the Bishops of Lichfield and Coventry; the estate was later acquired by the Anson family in 1625, which held it until the 20th century (National Trust). The most renowned member of the Anson family was George Anson, who was born at Shugborough in 1697. He was a distinguished admiral and circumnavigator, best known for his voyage around the world from 1740 to 1744. George Anson joined the Royal Navy in 1712 and rose through the ranks, becoming a captain in 1737. In 1740, he was appointed commodore of a squadron of six ships to attack Spanish-held possessions in the Pacific Ocean. George Anson's voyage was a significant undertaking. The crew was afflicted by disease, and storms damaged Anson's ships badly. However, he eventually captured a Spanish treasure galleon, the *Nuestra Señora de Covadonga*, carrying a large amount of silver. George Anson ultimately circumnavigated the globe and returned to England with a great deal of treasure. Anson's voyage made him a national hero, and he was rewarded with a peerage and a position as First Lord of the Admiralty. Anson died in 1762 and was buried in Colwich Church, Staffordshire. He is considered one of the most influential figures in British Naval History. Upon George's passing, his elder brother, Thomas, inherited his wealth and estates. Although trained as a lawyer, Thomas is thought to have never practiced law and instead traveled the world. His worldly travels inspired his improvements to the grounds surrounding the Shugborough estate (Pennant).

Shugborough Hall is a beautiful historic estate that testifies to the Anson family's wealth and influence and reminds us of George Anson's remarkable achievements. The Lanthorn of Demosthenes Monument, constructed 1764-1771, replicates a classical ruin that architect James Athenian Stuart sketched on his travels. The original Lanthorn of Demosthenes was modeled after the Choragic Monument of Lysicrates, which stands near the Acropolis in Athens and dates back to 4 BC, the time of Alexander the Great. The monument is also known as the Dark Lantern. It is a drum-shaped structure with engaged Corinthian columns, a domed top surmounted by a gilded cauldron beacon, and stands with gilded scrolls and dolphin supporters (Baker).

The Doric Temple at Shugborough is a folly built in the 1760s by the architect James Stuart, who was inspired by the Temple of Hephaestus in Athens. The temple is made of white Hollington stone and is a peripteral temple with a portico of six columns. The pediment is decorated with a relief of the Three Graces and is a beautiful example of Georgian architecture (Baker).

Doric Temple at Shugborough
(Brooker)

The Chinese House is inspired by George Anson's travels to China during his circumnavigation of the globe in the 1740s and is one of England's earliest examples of Chinese-style architecture. The Chinese house, circa 1747, is rectangular and has a pyramidal roof and a pagoda-like finial. The walls are plastered,

Chinese House at Shugborough
(Brooker)

and the windows are elaborately fenestrated. The interior had a fine plaster ceiling, which had been removed from the hall in the 19th century (Baker).

The Cat's Monument is located on the grounds of Shugborough Hall. It is a tall pedestal supporting a stone urn, and a life-size cat statue is on top. The monument was designed by Thomas Wright of Durham and was built in 1749-1750. The monument is situated to the north of the house; it is made of Coade stone and consists of a rectangular pedestal supporting a stone urn surmounted by the figure of a cat

Cat's Monument at Shugborough (Brooker)

that looks towards Shepherd's Monument. The purpose of the monument is still being determined. There are two theories. It commemorates a cat that traveled around the world with Admiral George Anson on his circumnavigation voyage in the 1740s, or it's to Kouli-Khan, a Persian cat owned by Thomas Anson, the nephew of Admiral Anson (Baker).

The Shepherd's Monument, a masterpiece of art and architecture, was erected between 1748 and 1763 on the grounds of Shugborough Hall. This small, Doric temple-like structure houses a relief of Nicolas Poussin's celebrated painting *The Arcadian Shepherds*, also known as *Et in Arcadia Ego*. The relief beautifully depicts a woman and three shepherds, two pointing towards a tomb.

Shepherd's Monument at Shugborough
(Brooker)

Carved on the tomb are the words *Et in Arcadia Ego*, which in Latin means "I (death), am present in Arcadia."

Beneath the relief is a mysterious inscription that has yet to be decoded. The inscription consists of O U O S V A V V, between and above the letters D and M. The inscription's meaning has been the subject of much speculation, and there have been many attempts to decipher it. Some theories suggest it is a coded message, while others believe it references a particular person or event and has been called one of the world's top uncracked ciphertexts (Baker).

Chapter Three
Artisans of the Shepherd's Monument
O·U·O·S·V·A·V·V

D·   M·

To fully comprehend the message of the *Shepherd's Monument*, it is crucial to understand the artisans who crafted it, their lives, and their skills. Were they portraying the values of their patrons, condemning their excesses, or entwining their own stories into the stone? Our objective is to interpret the true intention and significance of the monument by immersing ourselves in the cultural context, the craftsmanship of the artisans, and the cryptic message conveyed in the inscriptions.

According to various researchers, the monument dates from 1748 to 1767. The most commonly accepted explanation for the structure's curious nature is that it is a work by Thomas Wright from 1748 to 1750, with additional contributions by James Stuart around 1763 (Baker).

"The monument can be considered as having three distinct parts, each of which may have had a separate designer whose work could date from different years. There is a rustic arch in stone, carved to look wild and natural; within this arch is a white marble frame which supports a bas-relief based on Poussin's painting – this depicts three shepherds alongside a tomb, one standing and two kneeling, both of whom are both pointing out the tomb's inscription to a female figure standing calmly to one side" (Baker).

The sketch to the right is an early incarnation of the Shepherd's Monument, which Thomas Wright drew.

(Wright)

Later, columns were added to the Shepherd's Monument, discovered in drawings at the British Museum. James Athenian Stuart created these drawings. Although the columns resemble the rustic ones on the Shepherd's Monument, it is still being determined that the Shepherd's Monument columns were attributed to Stuart (Baker).

Finally, Peter Scheemakers sculpted *Et in Arcadia Ego*. Thomas Anson commissioned the Shepherd's Monument, designed by Thomas Wright and possibly James Stuart and sculpted by Peter Scheemakers.

Peter Scheemakers, a Flemish artist who worked in England in the 18th century, was the sculptor of the marble relief that copied Poussin's painting *Et in Arcadia Ego*, a reverse replica of *The Arcadian Shepherds*. Scheemakers was the principal sculptor, a Dutchman who worked in England in the early 1748-1750s. He was also known for his Shakespeare and Locke statues in Westminster Abbey. "The eight letters themselves, OUOSVAVV, are not attested before 1817 but are said to have been there at the time of Thomas Anson's death" (Mitchell).

"The Shepherd's Monument has a complicated history: the original white marble bas-relief by Scheemakers was later given a frame of stone carved in a rustic manner, and later again, the whole was placed in a Doric aedicule, probably designed in the 1760s by Stuart. This continual reworking suggests to me that Anson may have been largely responsible for their design himself and that he picked up and incorporated ideas from pattern books and from buildings seen on his travels that appealed to him without necessarily consulting any of the architects who originally conceived the motifs" (Kingsley).

A differing insight by Andrew Baker, author of *Thomas Anson of Shugborough and The Greek Revival*, references the possible source of the Shepherd's Monument design.

"Wright as the architect of the first phase of developments at Shugborough is based on the similarity of the Shepherd's Monument to one of Wright's drawings. In Wright's published book of designs for arbors, the first of an intended series of three volumes of *Universal Architecture* in 1755, one of his drawings resembles the shape of the rough stone arch in which the relief is placed" (Baker).

The classical style of ancient Rome and Greece influenced Scheemakers. He created many works of art for the aristocracy and the public in England. The Scheemakers Shugborough shepherd sculpture replicates *Et in Arcadia Ego*, painted by Nicolas Poussin from 1637 to 1638. The painting depicts a group of shepherds discovering a tomb with the inscription *Et in Arcadia Ego*, which means even in Arcadia, death is present. The phrase *Et in Arcadia Ego* has been interpreted in many different ways over the centuries. Some people see it as a reminder of the fragility of life, while others see it as a reminder that death is a natural part of life. It has also been interpreted as a commentary on the human condition or a reflection on the nature of art and beauty. No matter how it is interpreted, the phrase *Et in Arcadia Ego* is a powerful and evocative reminder of the inevitability of death. It reminds us that even in the most perfect places, there is always something to remind us of our mortality.

The Shepherd's Monument features a marble replica of the artwork *Et In Arcadia Ego;* however, the sculpture is believed to have been created reversely due to an error during the drawing transfer process. Thomas Anson, the owner of the estate where the monument is located, left no paper trail related to his personal life or the improvements to Shugborough Hall, indicating a desire to keep his life secret. It is presumed that the sculptor Scheemaker was instructed to create fingers pointing to the letters N and R without any explanation provided by Anson. Detailed instructions would have also been given by Anson to the artisans regarding the ten-letter inscription carved onto the plaque and the precisely placed dots that followed each letter. Thomas Wright, an architect and astronomer, was also unaware of the hidden meaning of DOUOSVAVVM encrypted on the plaque. The inscription dots, which, when decrypted, are connected to the work Wright did in astronomy. The timeline of creating the ten-letter plaque aligns differently with the early development of the Shugborough grounds. Still, the plaque was created simultaneously or later when Thomas Wright wrote *An Original Theory* in 1750. The geometric solution to the nine dots reveals a graphic drawn by Wright within the pages of *An Original Theory.* As for Scheemaker, Wright, and Stuart, I assert that none of them were made aware of the inscription's meaning and were commissioned to produce the monument per Thomas Anson's instructions.

Chapter Four
Shepherd's Inscription Solution
O·U·O·S·V·A·V·V

D·   M·

Step into the opulent world of Shugborough Estate, where sunlight danced through grand windows in the 18th century. Laughter and the clinking of teacups fill the air as aristocratic guests engage in a lively battle of wits. Their conversation, peppered with intellectual jousting and wordplay, reveals a fashionable pastime: anagrams.
These intricate puzzles weren't just child's play, where rearranging letters unlocks hidden words. They were a playground for the affluent, a way to showcase mental prowess and impress peers. Even crowned heads weren't immune to their allure.

King Louis XIII of France employed Thomas Billon as his royal anagram artist, tasked with crafting playful linguistic feats for the court (Blake).

Anagrams weren't merely frivolous entertainment. They held the potential for far more. Sir Francis Bacon, a renowned thinker, used them to cloak his profound philosophical insights, creating a layer of secrecy that intrigued and frustrated scholars for centuries.

Across the English Channel, Galileo Galilei, gazing at the heavens, made a groundbreaking discovery: rings around Saturn. To avoid unwanted attention, he ingeniously encoded this revelation in an anagram within a letter to a powerful duke. Only those with keen minds and a taste for puzzles could unlock his celestial secret (Gebler).

Robert Hooke used a playful cipher to conceal his profound insight into Hooke's Law. He first announced his spring law in 1676, publishing it as an anagram and giving the letters "cediinnoopssttuu." Two years later, he answered the puzzle—the letters were rearranged to spell "Ut Pondus sic Tensio," which means "as the extension, so the weight" (Chapman).

Even Isaac Newton, the enigmatic genius, dabbled in the art. He concealed groundbreaking theories on light and gravity using anagrams in his scientific writings. These intricate puzzles became testaments to his brilliance, challenging future generations to decipher his hidden truths (Biot).

These scientists' masterful use of anagrams secured their place in scientific history and revealed a hidden layer of creativity within their brilliant minds.

These are just a few examples of how anagrams transcended mere social games, becoming tools for personal expression, scientific intrigue, and even coded messages.

For over 270 years, the Shepherd Inscription, a ten-letter enigma, has baffled minds as brilliant as Darwin, Dickens, and Wedgewood. Could it hold the key to forgotten knowledge or a playful challenge from a bygone era? The mystery waits, beckoning those who dare to unlock its secrets.

The most recent Shugborough Inscription solution was proposed in 2014 by Keith Massey, a Latin teacher and former analyst for the NSA, who interprets eight of the ten Shugborough Inscription letters OUOSVAVV as an Initialism. Each letter represents a Latin word, forming a Latin phrase, Oro Ut Omnes Sequantur Viam Ad Veram Vitam, translated as I pray that all may follow the Way to True Life. Massey believes the Latin phrase is similar to *John 14:6*; I am the way, and the truth, and the life (Kinley). Massey's decipherment also addressed the second line or the lower letters D and M, representing a Roman funerary marking Dis Manibus, translated as dedicated to the shades (Kockley).

Ultimately, judging the 'correctness' of a solution remains subjective and depends on various factors beyond just linguistic mechanics.

My solution for the ten letters DOUOSVAVVM contains mixed-letter word anagram and composite-letter initialism. The mixed-letter anagram ADSUM is created from the letters DUSAM, and the initialism is formed from OOVVV. The solution to DOUOSVAVVM has a simple Latin word and initialism at its heart. The first step is recognizing two lines or levels—the upper OUOSVAVV and the lower letters D M.

Vanity Of Vanities All is Vanity
Vanitas Of Vanitatum Omnia Vanitas

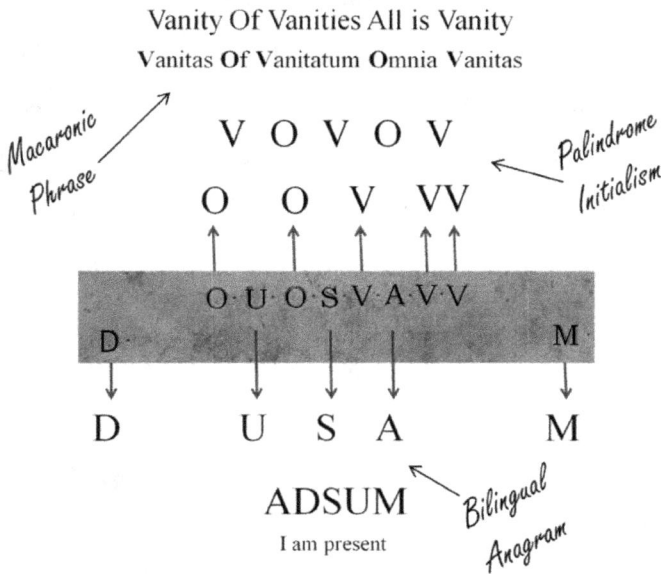

Moving the letters U S A to the lower line with the letters D M creates the Slavic word D U S A M; dušam is an old-world Slavic word defined as soul or spirit. Modern Slovenian uses dusa for the word soul. The word dušam is found in older Slovenian text, which appears in the following verses from a Slavic passage: "Anhela mirna, v'irna nastavnika, chranitefa **dušam** i t'ilom našim, u Hospoda prosim" (Annunciation Byzantine Catholic Church). Translation: O peaceful and faithful teacher, protect our **souls** and bodies; I pray to the Lord. Another example is "Dobrych i olemych **dušam** našim, i mira mirovi, u Hospoda prosim" (Annunciation Byzantine Catholic Church). Translated: For the good and pious **souls** of ours, and for peace in the world, I pray to the Lord. Another example of the use of dušam in a Slavic prayer from the manuscript *Oral Traditions*: "Narna bog dô zdravlje i veselje, mrtvim **dušam**" (Kleut). Translated: May God give health and happiness to the living, eternal salvation to the dead **souls**.

DUSAM is an anagram of the Latin ADSUM, meaning "I am present." Nicolas Poussin famously used this phrase in his painting *Et In Arcadia Ego*, in the Shepherd's Monument, which translates to "even in Arcadia, there am I," or in the context of the Shepherd's Monument, "I am present." When the letters in DUSAM become ADSUM,

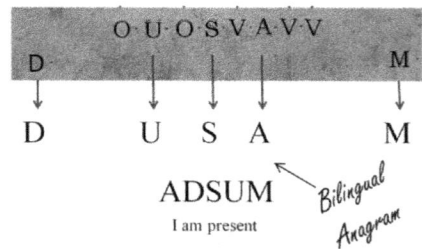

28

together, they represent the presence of a soul or spirit at the Shepherd's Monument. It is possible that the word dušam, a Slavic term which means soul or spirit, included on the Shepherd's Inscription solution as an anagram of the Latin word adsum could have been introduced to Thomas Anson during his travels across Europe and Greece or found in one of the many books in his library. Additionally, the word dušam may have been introduced in conversation by an immigrant laborer working at Shugborough Hall while constructing one of its many projects.

Latin was a prominent language of instruction in 18th-century England, especially in elite schools. The British School teacher reads the class register attendance, calls the student's name, and the student replies, adsum (Thornton) (Aylward).

The Christian religion defines adsum as my spirit is present to do your will (Sabatier). *Adsum* is also the title of a monthly Catholic journal published by the seminarians of Mater Dei Seminary.

The religious reverence of Adsum/Dusam dovetails nicely into Poussin's stone relief of the *Et in Arcadia Ego*, which many interpret as a representation of the Latin Memento Mori. Remember, you must die.

Vanity Of Vanities All is Vanity
Vanitas Of Vanitatum Omnia Vanitas

Macaronic Phrase →

V O V O V

O O V VV

← Palindrome Initialism

O·U·O·S·V·A·V·V

D   M

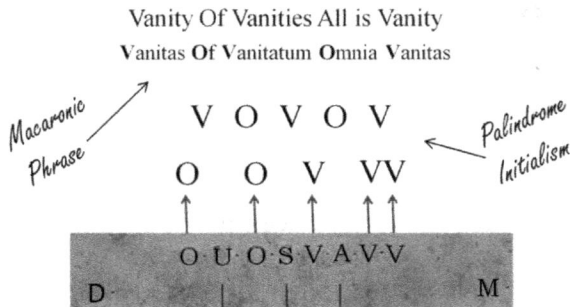

The letters OOVVV can be unscrambled and rearranged to form the wordplay Initialism-palindrome VOVOV, which stands for Vanitas Of Vanitatum Omnia Vanitas. Vanitas Of Vanitatum Omnia Vanitas combines Latin and English, where Of is an English word used with the Latin phrase. This phrase involves two languages and relates to a wordplay called a macaronic phrase (Dodd) (Päivi Pahta). Vanitas Of Vanitatum Omnia Vanitas translates to "Vanity Of Vanities All Is Vanity" in English. Another way to understand this is to accept that life is impermanent. Vanitas Of Vanitatum Omnia Vanitas, "Vanitas Vanitatum Omnia Vanitas" became known in the art world as the Vanitas genre. The Vanitas genre is interpreted by Flemish artists who create still-life paintings of human skulls with a collection of everyday items in the early 17th century. The Vanitas genre is a form of art that reflects on the inevitability of death and serves as a reminder of the transience of life. Peter Scheemakers, who sculpted the *Et In Arcadia Ego* on the Shugborough Shepherd's Monument, was partnered with sculptor Laurent Delvaux; they were in the business of sculpting funerary monuments in England. Laurent Delvaux sculpted

a marble Vanitas genre funerary monument statue of a putto cherub and a skull in 1750 (Delvaux). The partnership between Scheemakers and

(Delvaux)

Delvaux and the example of the cherub and skull from the Vanitas genre helped to establish a Latin and religious foundation for this interpretation of the Shugborough cipher (Shedd).

Chapter Five
Shepherd's Inscription Dot Solution
Saturn's Rings
O·U·O·S·V·A·V·V

D·   M·

A true Renaissance man, Thomas Wright of
Durham, 1711-1786, excelled in various fields. His work
spanned astronomy, mathematics, instrument making,
architecture, and garden design. Wright was Shugborough's
first architect hired by Thomas Anson. "Thomas Wright
came from a quite different place and social background.
He was the son of a yeoman carpenter in county Durham,
who, by sheer force of personality, found his way into high
society as a teacher of mathematical subjects to young
ladies" (Baker).

His most significant contributions lie in astronomy,
where he earned the title of the first modern cosmologist.
Wright conducted groundbreaking research by mapping the
Milky Way, proposing its spiral structure, and suggesting
that faint nebulae were distant galaxies. This revolutionary
idea, challenging the prevailing view of a single, unified
universe, laid the groundwork for our modern
understanding of the vast and intricate cosmos (Baker).

Beyond the cosmos, Wright's talents extended to other domains. He was a tutor for wealthy aristocrats; he crafted intricate architectural plans, designed serene gardens, and even authored historical texts. His life embodied the spirit of the Enlightenment, where curiosity and intellectual exploration flourished across various disciplines. While some of his accomplishments, like garden design, might be lesser known, they highlight his diverse skill set and insatiable thirst for knowledge (Baker).

There is very little documentation that Thomas Wright worked on monuments or gardens at Shugborough or letters of his friendship with Thomas Anson: "There is no evidence of the involvement of astronomer and architect Thomas Wright in the landscaping and building of the monuments and the extensions to the house" (Baker).

"An important piece of evidence cited by Eileen Harris, in her identification of Thomas Wright as the architect of the first phase of developments at Shugborough, is based on the similarity of the Shepherd's Monument to one of Wright's drawings. In Wright's published book of designs for arbors, the first of an intended series of three volumes of *Universal Architecture* in 1755, one of his drawings resembles the shape of the rough stone arch where the relief is placed" (Baker).

Was Thomas Wright at Shugborough when he authored *An Original Theory?* In 1750, astronomer Thomas Wright rocked the scientific world with *An Original Theory*, proposing a radical new view of the cosmos. He envisioned our universe not as an infinite, uniform expanse but a giant island of stars resembling our Milky Way galaxy. This island universe housed countless stars scattered across a vast disc, with our sun near the edge. Wright's theory wasn't just based on philosophical musings. He used telescopic observations to support his claims, explaining the Milky Way's appearance and the absence of stars in specific directions. He even employed mathematical calculations to estimate the universe's size and structure. While limited by his understanding of nebulae (later known as distant galaxies), Wright's model laid the foundation for the island universe concept, which Edwin Hubble later confirmed in the 20th century. His work influenced giants like Kant and Herschel, shaping cosmological thought and sparking scientific interest through innovative illustrations and clear explanations. Though not entirely accurate, *An Original Theory* remains a significant milestone, offering a daring vision of the universe that paved the way for modern understanding

(Wright, *An Original Theory or New Hypothesis of The Universe*).

Wright's most notable contribution was his explanation that the Milky Way is a galaxy seen from its outer edge as a river of stars. As Wright explained, Kant took up this concept in Europe, though only partially. As Wright explained, Immanuel Kant saw the reality of the galaxy more correctly than Wright understood it. Still, Wright's ideas had opened up astronomy to consider patterns and structures far vaster than the Earth's solar system.

Thomas Wright's book *An Original Theory* features a series of images referenced as plates at the end of the book. Plate XXVIII, fig. III illustrates the planet Saturn.

Thomas wrote in *An Original Theory* regarding Saturn, "The manner of Saturn's

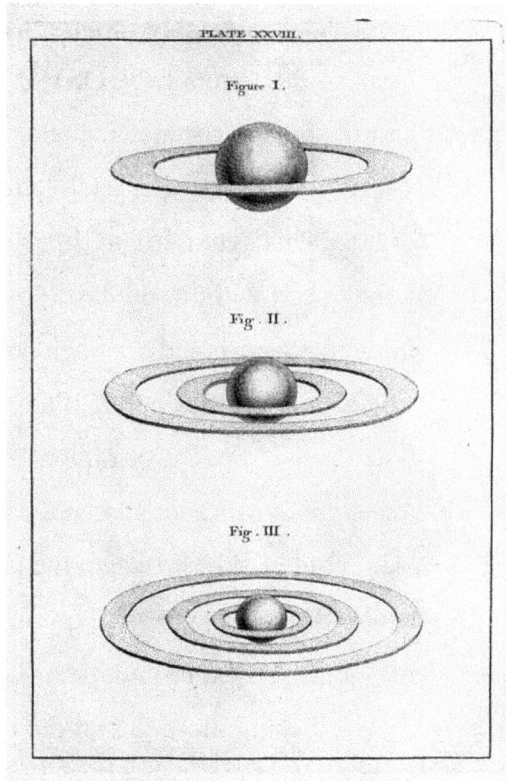

(Wright)

35

rings, nay perhaps ring within the ring to a third or fourth order as shown in Plate XXVIII nothing being more evident than that if all the Stars we see moved in one vast ring like those of Saturn round any central body or point the general phenomena of our Stars would be solved by it" (Wright, An Original Theory or New Hypothesis of The Universe).

The Shepherd's Monument has ten letters with nine distinct dots or points following each letter except the last letter, V. This display of letters and points conceals two ciphers, the letters DOUOSVAVVM, solved by wordplay and the dots, a geometric puzzle formed from the coordinate points after each letter.

This symmetrical display of letters and dots seemed unbalanced without the last letter, V, having a dot. I also noticed a near-equal distance between the O, S, and V dots. The S-dot is positioned halfway between the O-dot and V-dot. This symmetry, or rather, lack of it, was also unusual since the distances between the other letter dots were staggered or skewed when measuring outward from the center S dot. As we will explore, this unique arrangement of dots is critical to understanding the hidden ciphers.

Living more than three thousand miles from the monument, I have made my assessments from a

considerable number of photographs taken of the
inscription from various placements, including high-quality
frontal images provided by the National Trust.

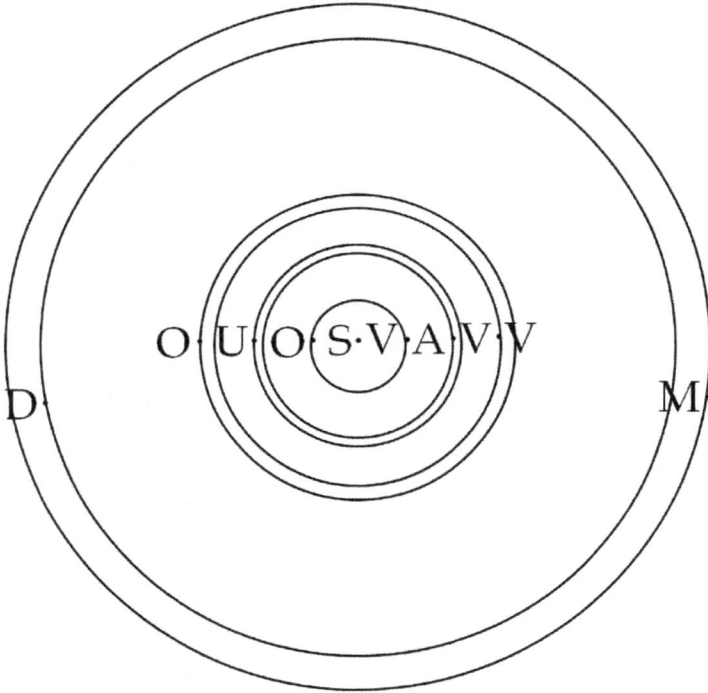

I also considered the possibility of image
perspective distortion skewing the distances between each
dot. The summation of all photographs measured produced
a consistent three-ring pattern with a center circle
representing Saturn. The Saturn rings and planet matches
Thomas Wright's drawing of Saturn in his book *An
Original Theory*. The three Shugborough Inscription rings

require only six dots. Each of the six dots is unevenly spaced from the center S dot, forming the width of the three rings. The dot puzzle brings to mind the adage that form follows function, as the sum of its parts serves a specific purpose to replicate Thomas Wright's illustration in *An Original Theory*.

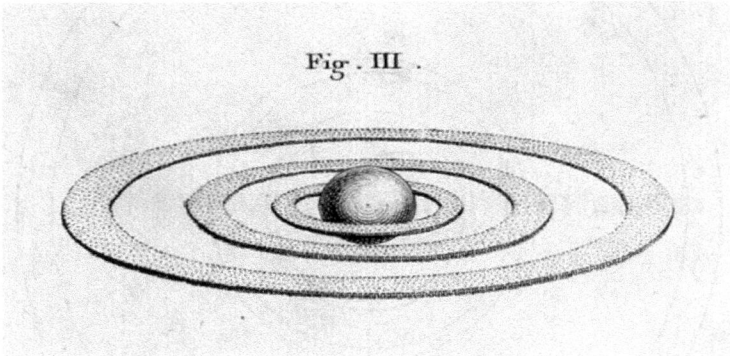

Fig . III .

(Wright)

I retrieved my drafting compass and drew circles using the letter S-dot as the center point. The first circle intersected the letters O-dot and V-dot, making a centered circle that became the planet Saturn. The following two letters are U-dot and A-dot, which make up the first inner ring of Saturn. Next, moving out to the letters O-dot and V-dot, we form the second ring of Saturn.

Lastly, the letters D-dot and M-dot form Saturn's outer ring. The final image is a top view of Saturn with three rings, depicted as a pictorial view by Thomas Wright in *An Original Theory*. The inscription's center letter, S, is an abbreviation for the planet Saturn.

I assume the dots arranged after each letter in a Saturn-like ringed planet shape on the Shepherd's Monument inscription are a tribute to Thomas Wright by Thomas Anson. I also assert that the encrypted dot solution was unknown to Thomas Wright or anyone else. The rationale for the dots that geometrically form Thomas Wright's illustration of the planet Saturn in his book *An Original Theory* was to eternalize Wright's legacy as an astronomer and architect and his work at Shugborough Hall. The memorialization of Thomas Wright on the Shepherd's Monument emphasizes the importance of Wright's unique relationship with Thomas Anson, which parallels his relationship with his brother George, who is also immortalized on the Shepherd's Monument encrypted in stone.

Chapter Six
Shepherd's Monument
Et In Arcadia Ego Solution
O·U·O·S·V·A·V·V

D·   M·

The Shepherd's Monument, with its plain-text ten-
letter inscription DOUOSVAVVM, has been a mystery at
Shugborough Hall for many years. This puzzle has
intrigued and challenged viewers to decipher it. My
proposed solution is a wordplay puzzle that is logical,
plausible, elusive, and difficult to prove definitively.

This inscription has sparked historical fascination
and serves a dual purpose. First, it bewilders and confounds
cryptographers, challenging
their intellect. Second,
it diverts attention from the
hidden puzzle within the *Et
In Arcadia Ego* inscription.
With its intricate elegance,
the Poussin tomb's cipher
lies at the heart of this enigma.

Nicolas Poussin, *Et In Arcadia Ego*, (Springer)

Nicolas Poussin's *Et In Arcadia Ego* chiseled onto
the tomb in the Poussin painting conceals a simple Latin
anagram: I Tego Arcana Dei, which translates to "Begone! I

41

Conceal God's Secrets". This phrase itself is perplexing. What kind of secret is being kept, and who is holding them?

The image to the right is an enlarged section of the *Et In Arcadia Ego* of the Nicolas Poussin painting.

Poussin strategically used multiple vanishing points within a composition to create a more dynamic and realistic depiction of space, especially to depict various receding

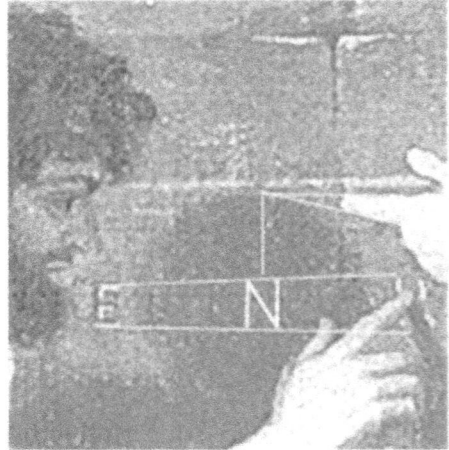

Nicolas Poussin, Et In Arcadia Ego, (Springer)

planes within the scene. By converging parallel lines towards a vanishing point on the horizon, Poussin creates the illusion of receding space, making the scene feel deeper than the flat canvas. The shepherd's extended finger acts as a compositional tool. It points directly at the tomb, likely the focal point of the painting. Since our eyes naturally follow the direction of a pointed finger, it guides our gaze deeper into the painting towards the vanishing point where the tomb resides. The finger reinforces the perspective and draws us into the scene.

The shepherd on the right side of the image extends a finger and points at the tomb. The finger's shape originates from a vanishing point on the tomb directly above the letter N in *Et In Arcadia Ego*. The N is also in the center of the shadow from the shepherd's head. The shepherd on the left side of the painting points to the letter R.

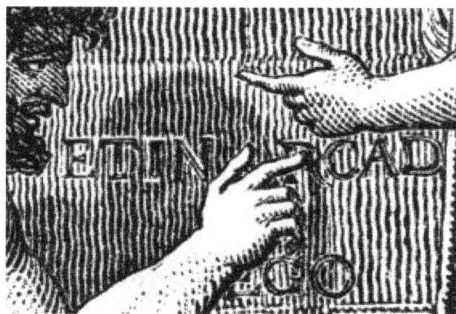
(Mathieu)

The etching to the right by Jean Mathieu accurately represents Nicolas Poussin's *Et In Arcadia Ego*, with the Shepherd on the left pointing to the letter R (Mathieu).

The Bernard Picart 1692 etching of *Et In Arcadia Ego* is reversed, with the shepherd pointing to the letter N instead of the letter R, as in the Poussin version (Picart).

(Picart)

The two etchings highlight the significance of "N" and "R" in *Et In Arcadia Ego*, unveiling a concealed meaning.

The Shugborough Hall Shepherd's Monument, adorned with Poussin's *Et in Arcadia Ego*, holds the key to unraveling the mystery behind the inscription and the monument's purpose.

The image of the two Shugborough Shepherd's fingers, each subtly pointing to the letters N and R, has captivated

Peter Scheemakers, *Et In Arcadia Ego*, (Wood)

solvers. This intriguing detail has led to the creation of various words from the encrypted initialism. Many solvers have approached the N-R puzzle by considering the addition of the letters N and R, mistakenly adding an extra layer of complexity to the solution. However, in truth, the N and R are not contributors but rather detractors.

Francis Bacon described the possibility of anagramic ciphers having more letters than needed to solve the cipher. In the case of the *Et in Arcadia Ego,* the extra letters are the letters N and R.

Bacon, in describing ciphers (and anagrams are ciphers), directs that nulls or extra letters shall be introduced for the purpose of mystifying the would-be decipherer. Such superfluities in no way disguise the true word from the understanding cryptographer. Additional letters could be added to an anagram, essentially creating an anagram cipher. The solution would only be known to the ones in the know (A Sub-Committee of the Bacon Society).

Let's delve into the heart of the matter. Taking the letters N and R from Poussin's *Et In Arcadia Ego*, we are left with the remaining sequence: *Et I_ A_ cadia Ego*. Recognizing that the Shepherd's Inscription was encoded using wordplay, we apply a similar approach to decipher it.

The solution is in an anagram: *Et I_ A_ cadia Ego*. Anagrams, at their pinnacle, transform words from one language into another.

From the remaining letters in *Et I_ A_ cadia Ego*, we extract the following:

1. **Deai**: This archaic Latin word translates to Goddess.
2. **Gaia**: A Greek word representing the ancient Greek Goddess symbolizing the Earth. Gaia is often depicted holding a sphere, signifying planet Earth.
3. **Ceto**: Another Greek deity, Ceto, is a primordial Sea Goddess in Greek mythology. She is the daughter of Pontus and Gaia, and her description often includes references to a sea monster.

Therefore, the anagrammatic solution to *Et I_ A_ cadia Ego* reveals the triumvirate: Deai, Gaia, and Ceto.

Deai is archaic Latin. In older forms of Latin, there was some fluidity in declensions, particularly for first declension nouns. This occasional alternate spelling of 'deai' was less common but still considered a grammatically acceptable form.

The Latin spelling of goddess is typically spelled Dea or Deae. An example of Deai as a Goddess is an inscription on a stone in Lanuvium, Italy: si deo si deai, translation: if God, if Goddess (Sandys).

But how does it relate to George Anson, the man for whom the Shepherd's Monument was erected?

After George Anson's passing, a memorial medal emerged around 1768, sparking speculation that Thomas

Anson designed it. On one side of the medal, an Admiral, George Anson, gazes forth from a bust image.

However, the reverse side holds genuine intrigue: a Goddess (Deai) gracefully perches on the back of a sea monster (Ceto) on an earth orb (Gaia).

In this delicate interplay of symbols, we catch glimpses of hidden narratives—the echoes of secrets whispered across time from the hands of Thomas Anson. The interplay begins with Poussin's enigmatic painting, *Et In Arcadia Ego*, whose inscription cryptically anagrammatically declares, I Keep God's Secrets. *Et In Arcadia Ego* metamorphoses further, evolving into the Shugborough Inscription *Et I_ A_ cadia Ego*, eventually

leading us to the anagrams Deai, Gaia, and Ceto. Finally, we arrive at the Thomas Anson-designed memorial medal tribute to his younger brother, Admiral George Anson, forming a secret circle of truth.

The George Anson bust side of the medal, note the wreath of victory above Admiral George Anson's head. Additionally, there are seven wreaths on the Deai, Gaia, and Ceto side of the medal. Peter Scheemaker's *Et in Arcadia Ego* carving on the Shepherd's Monument features an urn and wreath above the stone crypt. Notably,

Peter Scheemakers, *Et In Arcadia Ego*, (Barlow)

the urn and wreath are unique to Peter Scheemaker's version of *Et in Arcadia Ego* and were absent in Nicolas Poussin's original painting. The Scheemaker carved wreath placed in context with the eight wreaths on the Anson medal leads to the presumption that the carved urn and wreath from the Scheemaker's version of *Et in Arcadia Ego* representatively symbolizes Admiral George Anson's presents.

Art historians have often pondered the significance of the stoic shepherdess, who stands apart from the tomb in Poussin's *Et In Arcadia Ego*. Her presence, alongside the three shepherds, exudes Goddess-like qualities. Despite this, the lack of additional evidence leaves uncertainty about her true identity.

Alphonse Lamotte

The shepherdess in Poussin's *Et In Arcadia Ego* remains mysterious. Could she embody a divine figure, perhaps even Gaia, the Earth Goddess, as the embodiment of Earth, could represent the enduring and ever-present cycle of life and death? The cryptic anagram of the painting's title, I Keep God's Secrets, suggests a hidden spiritual dimension. Alternatively, the memorial medal commemorating Admiral George Anson's victory at Cape Finisterre offers a contrasting interpretation. Its imagery - the Goddess Victory (Deai) on a globe (Gaia), symbolizing triumph over the sea monster (Ceto) representing challenges - suggests the shepherdess might reflect Anson's

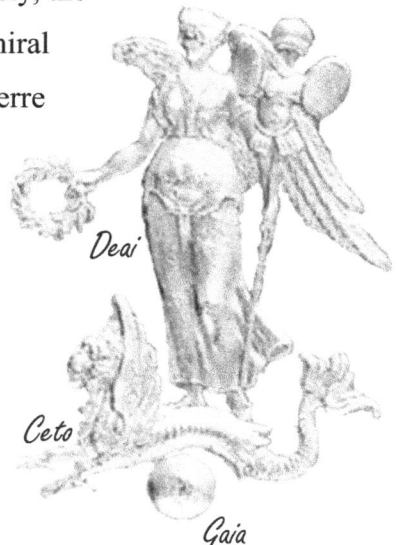

Deai

Ceto

Gaia

accomplishments and global journey.

Ultimately, exploring these diverse interpretations enriches our understanding of Poussin's painting, inviting us to contemplate the complexities of nature, mortality, and human ambition woven into its enigmatic imagery. The parallel between the George Anson memorial medal and the anagrammatic interpretation of *Et I_ A_cadia Ego* of Poussin's reverse sculpture on the Shepherd's Monument conveys together that both the memorial medal and sculpture were constructed to honor the distinguished triumphs of Admiral George Anson's life.

Conclusion
O·U·O·S·V·A·V·V
D·   M·

The Shugborough inscription, a ten-letter enigma known as DOUOSVAVVM, along with the enigmatic geometric dots and the haunting phrase *Et In Arcadia Ego*, were all incorporated into the Shepherd's Monument from Thomas Anson's mind. These carefully crafted elements are a testament to his dedication to honoring the extraordinary lives and accomplishments of his younger brother, Admiral George Anson, and his close confidante, Thomas Wright.

The intricate wordplay of DOUOSVAVVM, meaning we lived twice, poignantly reminds us of life's fleeting nature. It speaks to George's absence and the enduring presence of the soul beyond mortality. The geometric pattern of the strategically placed dots, a symbol of the designer's profound knowledge, reflects the time and effort devoted to creating a haven - a Shugborough Arcadia - for Thomas Anson by Thomas Wright. Finally, the inscription *Et In Arcadia Ego*, meaning even in Arcadia, I am present, adds another layer of meaning. It acknowledges the transience of life, even amidst idyllic settings like Arcadia, and celebrates George's vibrant life and adventurous spirit. However, the lingering emptiness following his death is a potent Memento Mori. Regardless of achievements or fame, this universal truth reminds us of the inevitable void left behind, endured by the living.

Thomas's meticulous reengineering of the Shepherd's Monument, transforming it into a cryptic and enduring tribute to his brother, attempts to overcome this emptiness, the vacuum of forgetfulness. He strives to cheat death and preserve George's legacy by weaving hidden messages into the monument. He reminds us all that regardless of our station in life, we ultimately return to dust, leaving behind our physical presence and the echoes of our accomplishments.

Shugborough Inscription Wordplay for the Lords and Ladies is not just a historical analysis but also my journey of discovery, revealing my limited awareness of George Anson and his extraordinary adventures. This book is a testament to Thomas's unwavering commitment to immortalizing his brother's story, a reminder of the enduring power of remembrance in the face of mortality. We can only hope that our loved ones remember us fondly and create lasting memories, much like the enduring testament to Admiral George Anson's legacy embodied in the Shepherd's Inscription by his brother Thomas.

Works Cited

A Sub-Committee of the Bacon Society. *Baconiana.* London: Robert Banks and Son, 1803. Digital.

Ancient-Symbols.com. *Kingfisher.* 13 2 24. Digital. 13 2 24.

Annunciation Byzantine Catholic Church. *The Divine Liturgy of Our Father Saint John Chrysostom in Church Slavonic* . Anaheim: Annunciation Byzantine Catholic Church, 2007. Digital.

Aylward, Rev. A. F. "Adsum." *The N Z School Journal, Volume 16* (1922): 254-256. Digital.

Baker, Andrew. *Thomas Anson of Shugborough and The Greek Revival.* NA: Self Published, 2020. PDF.

Barlow, Paul. *Photograph of image at Shugorough hall copy of Poussin's Arcadia Shepherds.* Creative Commons Public Domain. *Photograph of image at Shugorough hall copy of Poussin's Arcadia Shepherds.* 2006. Digital.

Bell, Bethan. "The rise, fall, and rise of the status pineapple." 2 8 2020. *BBC.com.* Digital. 18 9 2023.

Biot, Jean Baptiste. *Life of Sir Isaac Newton.* Oxford: Oxford University, 1829. Digital.

Blake, Barry J. *SecretLanguage.* Oxford: Oxford University Press, 2010. Digital.

Brain, Jessica. *Rise and Fall of the English Stately Home.* 19 August 2021. Digital. 20 9 2023.

Brooker, Paul. "Shugborough Lanthorn of Demosthenes, Cats Monument, Doric Temple, Shepherd's Monument, Chinese House." *Paul Brooker (cc-by-sa/2.0), (Creative Commons Licence)*. Staffordshire, England: Paul Brooker, 30 June 2010. Digital.

Callender, G. A. R. *Sea Kings of Britain*. London: Longmans, Green, and Co., 1909. Digital.

Celje, Škofija. *Župnije Trbovlje-sv. Martin, Trbovlje-sv. Marija, Hrastnik in Dol pri Hrastniku*. 15 Marca 2012. Digital. 23 2 2024.

Chapman, Allan. *England's Leonardo Robert Hooke and the Seventeenth-Century Scientific Revolution*. London: Institute of Physics Publishing, , 2005. Digital.

Cook, Monte. *The Skeptic's Guide To Conspiracies*. Avon: Adams Media, an imprint of Simon and Schuster, Inc, 2009. Digital.

Delvaux, Laurent. *putto cherub and a skull* . Kollenburg Antiquairs. *Marble Vanitas Statue, attributed to Laurent Delvaux*. Postbus 171 NL-5688 ZK Oirschot The Netherlands, 2024. Digital.

Dirk Moosbach. *WordSense Online Dictionary*. 12 February 2024. Digital. 12 February 2024.

Dodd, Elizabeth S. *The Lyric Voice in English Theology*. London: Bloomsbury Publishing, 2023. Digital.

Gebler, Karl Von. *Galileo Galilei*. London: C.Kegan Paul and Co., 1879. Digital.

Helden, Albert Van. *Saturn and his Anses*. 1995. Digital. 24 2 2024.

John Denison Champlin, Charles Callahan Perkins. *Cyclopedia of Painters and Paintings*. New York: Charles Scribner's Sons, 1885-1886. Digital.

Jones and Co. *Jones' Views of the Seats, Mansions, Castles, Etc. of Noblemen and Gentlemen in England*. London: Jones & Co., Temple of the Muses, Finsbury Square, 1829. Digital.

Kingsley, Nick. *Landed Families of Britain and Ireland*. 10 12 2014. digital. 30 9 2023.

Kinley, Jeff. *Uncovering The Secrets Of Bible Prophecy*. Eugene: Harvest House, 2018. Digital.

Kleut, Marija. "Concluding Formulas of Audience Address in Serbo-Croatian Oral Epic." *Oral Tradition*. Slavica Publishers, Inc., May-October 1991. Digital.

Kockley, Mike. *200-year-old mystery of Shugborough Code 'solved'*. 21 December 2014. Digital. 12 February 2024.

Konstantīns Karulis. *Latviešu etimoloģijas vārdnīca: P-Ž*. Latvian: Avots, 1992. Digital.

Lamotte, Alphonse. *Et In Arcadia Ego*. Engraving.

Mallett, Alfred Williams and Walter Henry. *Mansions and Country Seats of Staffordshire and Warwickshire*. Lichfield: Frederic Brown, 1899. Digital.

Mathieu, Jean. *The Arcadian Shepherds (Et in Arcadia Ego)*. Philadelphia Museum of Art, Paris. Etching.

Mitchell, Jack. *Antigone Journal / Shug Days: Cracking A 270-Year-Old Epigraphical Mystery*. 28 4 2022. Digital. 20 2 2024.

Moffat, Ms H. "Pineapple Mania." *Tickhill History Society*. South Yorkshire: media.tickhillhistorysociety.org.uk, 10 8 2017. Digital.

National Trust. *History of Shugborough Estate*. n.d. Digital. 2 3 2024.

Newman, William R. *Princeton University Press, William R. Newman on Newton the Alchemist*. 7 November 2018. Digital. 24 2 2024.

Nicholls, Robert. *Secret Stafford*. Amberley Publishing, 2018. Digital.

Päivi Pahta, Janne Skaffari, Laura Wright. *Multilingual Practices in Language History: English and Beyond*. Boston / Berlin: De Gruyter Mouton, 2018.

Pennant, Thomas. *The Journey from Chester to London*. London: B. White, Fleet Street, 1782. Digital.

Picart, Bernard. *Le Souvenir De La Mort Au Milieu Des Prosperitez De La Vie*. The British Museum. *Et In Arcadia Ego*. Paris, 1688-1733. Etching.

Sabatier, Paul. *Life of St. Francis of Assisi*. New York: Charles Scribner's Sons, 1902. Digital.

Sandys, Sir John Edwin. *Latin Epigraphy, An Introduction to the Study of Latin Inscriptions*. Cambridge: University Press, 1919. Digital.

Scheong. "Throughout History." 8 13 2018. *The Rise and Fall of the Great Country Houses*. Digital. 18 9 2023.

Shedd, Julia A. *Famous Sculptors and Sculpture*. Boston and New York: The Riverside Press, Cambridge, 1896. Digital.

Shortz, William F. "British Word Puzzles (1700-1822)." *Wordways 6, No.3* (1973): 131-38. Digital.

Smith, Kate. *Shugborough Case Study: The Mansion House*. 2014. Digital. 7 4 2024.

Springer, Anton. *The Renaissance in the North and the art of the 17th and 18th centuries*. Leipzig Saxony Germany: E. A. Seemann, 1878. Digital.

Tenison, Edward King. "Arch of Hadrian at Shugborough." https://www.search.staffspasttrack.org.uk/Details.aspx?&ResourceID=1656&PageIndex=3&SearchType=2&ThemeID=97, (1805-1878). Digital.

Thornton, Katharine. *The Messages of Its Walls and Fields: A History of St Peter's College.* West Kent Twon: The Council of Governors of St Peter's College, 2010. Digital.

Wood, Edward. *Shugborough Shepherds Monument, Fingers Pointing to Letters, close-up. Creative Commons Attribution-ShareAlike 3.0 License Self-published work.* 2011. Digital.

Wright, Thomas. *An Original Theory or New Hypothesis of The Universe.* London: H. Chapelle, 1750. Digital.

—. *Arbours & Grottos.* London: Act of Parliament, 1711-1786. Digital.

www.ingramcontent.com/pod-product-compliance
Lightning Source LLC
Chambersburg PA
CBHW060522280326
41933CB00014B/3063